The
Thingamabob

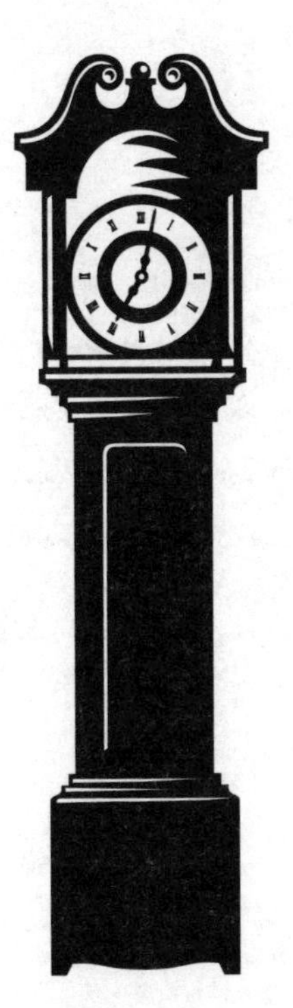

Mark Dever

The Christmas Thingamabob

Published by 10Publishing, a division of 10ofthose.com

9D Centurion Court, Farington, Leyland, PR25 3UQ, England

Email: info@10ofthose.com Website: www.10ofthose.com

ISBN 9781909611276

Reprinted once

Typeset and designed by Mike Thorpe www.design-chapel.com

Printed in the UK by CPI Group (UK) Ltd, Croydon, CR0 4YY

The Christmas Thingamabob

It was just a few days until Christmas, and Tom had looked long and hard for a gift for Sarah. Finally, he thought he had found it. Of all places, he discovered it up in the attic. He didn't quite know what it was, but it was very pretty and he thought it would look nice on the mantel above the fireplace. It looked like it was made out of brass, but it was only a few inches high and definitely needed polishing. He took it, put it in his pocket and snuck downstairs.

Later that evening, as Sarah was wrapping presents in the other room, he quietly polished it until it glistened. Picking out some special wrapping paper, he too wrapped his gift, added a small bow to it, with a card, and wrote on it Sarah's name. He placed it under the tree ready for Christmas morning.

Christmas morning came, and they exchanged their gifts. Sarah was always happy to receive presents at Christmas, and this one she particularly liked. 'Beautiful' and 'just the thing' were some of the words that came to her lips, but then she had said this about most of the gifts she had received that morning. Finally, after she had gazed at it enthusing for a few moments, she paused and asked Tom, 'But what is it?'

'It's a . . . thingamabob,' he said quickly. 'Let's just call it a thingamabob.'

Prepared for this question, Tom replied, 'I thought you might ask that. I'm not entirely sure. I think it is part of some old ornament or pipe or tool or something, but I think it would look pretty nice on the mantel.'

'But what is it, Tom?'

Again, Tom paused, slightly irritated.

'It's a . . . thingamabob,' he said quickly. 'Let's just call it a thingamabob.'

As she looked at it, and sounding out the words silently on her lips, Sarah hesitated and then said with a smile, 'OK, it's a thingamabob. We'll put it right over here.'

Sliding her hand along the mantel, knocking aside some of the Christmas cards they had received, Sarah made space for the thingamabob, placing it right in the middle. A Christmas tradition had been born. Tom had shined the brass up and it looked pretty festive with the red and green trimmings around it on the mantel, and whenever anyone asked them what it was, they simply said, 'a thingamabob'.

Sarah made space for the thingamabob, placing it right in the middle. A Christmas tradition had been born.

What Sarah had really wanted for Christmas that year was at least several hundred pounds more than the thingamabob had cost and several hundred pounds beyond what Tom's slender salary would allow.

A number of years ago, Sarah's parents had given her a beautiful grandfather clock, actually built by her grandfather. It was tall, a bit rustic, but beautifully carved and polished. Sarah always remembered it. It had been in her grandfather's house at the top of the stairs like it was guarding them, regularly ticking and tocking the time and chiming every quarter hour. She listened to it, stared at it, watched her grandfather wind it, played by it and with it, and one time, much to her grandfather's alarm, made it into a doll house! In short, she loved it and what she had really wanted for Christmas this year was for that clock to work. You see, it hadn't worked since it had been moved from her grandfather's house several

She loved it and what she had really wanted for Christmas this year was for that clock to work.

years before. A number of members of the family had looked at it in the years since. Neighbours had poked at it, but no one had succeeded in figuring out the problem.

It was a few years later that a most amazing thing happened with Sarah's clock.

So a few months ago, Tom had phoned two places that worked on grandfather clocks. He described the clock and the problem. Both places assured him that they could almost certainly make the clock work, but both also told him that the cost would certainly be several hundred dollars. That was hundreds of dollars more than Tom and Sarah had, and so Sarah's grandfather's clock stayed standing there silently.

It was a few years later that a most amazing thing happened with Sarah's clock. Andy, a friend of Tom's from work, was at their house helping them to set up some Christmas decorations in time for friends coming over later that evening. As he had every time before when he had come into their house, Andy spent a few moments looking at the grandfather clock, opening the door, pulling at this part, pushing at that one, then just shaking his head.

'I'm sure you could get that to work, Tom,' he said.

'So am I,' said Tom, 'but we don't have the money right now just to try.'

It was right after he said that that Tom bent down and took the thingamabob out of its box. He had had it professionally cleaned since that first year he had given it to Sarah, and each year they had come to like it more and more. It was something that somehow seemed to fit, though they didn't really understand what it was. When people would ask them about it, they could do no more than look at each other, smile, and say together, 'It's a thingamabob!' One time, the wife of one of Tom's friends even offered to buy it from them, so that she could use it in her decorations. It had become a part of their Christmas celebrations.

Tom bent down and took the thingamabob out of its box.

As Tom began to put the thingamabob on the mantel, Andy stared at it and asked him what it was.

As Tom began to put the thingamabob on the mantel, Andy stared at it and asked him what it was.

'Just a thingamabob,' said Tom.

'Where did you get it?' said Andy, feeling the object.

Tom told him the story of finding it in the attic one Christmas a few years back when they were particularly hard-up, polishing it, giving it to Sarah, and its subsequent life as a 'thingamabob' on their mantel every December. Andy stood looking at it for a moment, then he said, 'Do you mind if I try something with this? It might scratch it up a bit.'

Tom looked at him strangely, 'No,' he said.

'Help me lay the clock down on its side first,' said Andy.

About an hour later, there was no more thingamabob on the mantel. The thingamabob was back where it belonged and Sarah's grandfather's clock was finally working again – thanks to the thingamabob.

Born a little baby, amid hushed silence in a manger, some place with camels and wise men and shepherds.

For many people, the celebration of Christmas that we have in our culture is a bit like that thingamabob. Found in the attic of family tradition, having some beauty about it, over the years acquiring a certain amount of sentimental attachment, not so useful, but appreciated. I think this is probably because Jesus is a bit like that for many people. Born a little baby, amid hushed silence in a manger, some place with camels and wise men and shepherds. Angelic promises of peace, and a mystery star in the sky. Here is that birth scene as one writer in *The New York Times* put it a few years ago:

> *Christmas in Bethlehem. The ancient dream: a cold clear night made brilliant by a glorious star, the smell of incense, shepherds and wise*

men falling to their knees in adoration of the sweet baby, the incarnation of perfect love. This simple tableau is so rich with meaning that whether represented on the mantelpiece or in the mind, it seems suspended, complete unto itself, somewhere in eternity. [1]

Yet Christmas is not simply a celebration of human birth, with all the mystery, pain, hope and joy there is in that. This is a celebration of one particular birth and, if I could be forgiven for asking, what is the big deal about this birth? Why should we celebrate this birth as particularly as we do? Other people have been born in much more rustic settings. Other people have been born with more pomp and ceremony. Why does this birth excite people so that angels come, wise men travel and there's even a celestial sign? As the carols go: why should 'heaven and nature sing'? Why should 'Joyful, all ye nations, rise'? [2] All because of *this* baby.

Why should 'heaven and nature sing'? Why should 'Joyful, all ye nations, rise'?

So who is this baby?

History tells us some very specific details of Jesus' life. We're told of Jesus' birth, even before Mary is pregnant. His birth is detailed in a strangely deliberate way. We read in the Bible that Jesus wasn't here to be served, like a king; instead, He had come to serve others, and in doing so 'give his life as a ransom for many'. [3] The Bible tells us that Jesus is God's Son, sent by God 'to be the Saviour of the world' [4].

This is why there is great joy in Christmas. Not

just happiness at the thought of the season; the giving and receiving of nice gifts, eating good food and seeing friends and family, but a deep and real joy. Jesus comes with 'good news that will cause great joy'.[5]

But to answer the question of who Jesus is, we need to consider His adult life as well as His birth in that stable. He lived, worked and taught on earth for 33 years. And we might be surprised to read that rather than being a figure that united humanity with warm fuzzy feelings of Christmas joy, as traditions suggest, the real Jesus brought division. His identity was so significant that He provoked varying reactions amongst the people He encountered.

The real Jesus brought division. His identity was so significant that He provoked varying reactions amongst the people He encountered.

John, a disciple who wrote an eyewitness account of Jesus' life and death, records that Jesus Himself taught that He came from God.

In chapter 7 of John's Gospel, the main truth Jesus

taught was about Himself (you might like to read that chapter for yourself, which you will find at the end of this book). Verse 16 says: 'My teaching is not my own. It comes from the one who sent me.'

Jesus taught that God sent Him. That He came from God. Though the people of the day didn't realise it, Jesus fulfilled many Old Testament prophecies as He arrived on earth – God in human form. As verse 28 of this section says 'Then Jesus, still teaching in the temple courts, cried out, "Yes, you know me, and you know where I am from. I am not here on my own authority, but he who sent me is true. You do not know him, but I know him because I am from him and he sent me.' And when He says that *He* sent me, He means that He is from God. So Jesus fulfilled the prophecy of Micah chapter 5 verse 2: 'But you, Bethlehem Ephrathah, though you are small among the clans of Judah, out of you will come for me one who will be ruler over Israel,

Though the people of the day didn't realise it, Jesus fulfilled many Old Testament prophecies as He arrived on earth.

whose origins are from of old, from ancient times.'

Unlike you or me, this man existed before He was born; before He was conceived in the womb of the virgin Mary, He existed. And this fits with Jesus' teaching that He was going back to God. In verses 33 and 34 of this same chapter, Jesus said: 'I am with you for only a short time, and then I am going to the one who sent me. You will look for me, but you will not find me; and where I am, you cannot come.' Then the Jews said, in verses 35 and 36: 'Where does this man intend to go where we cannot find him? Will he go where our people live scattered among the Greeks, and teach the Greeks? What did he mean when he said, "You will look for me, but you will not find me," and "Where I am, you cannot come"?'

What did he mean when he said, "You will look for me, but you will not find me,"?'

Jesus told them that His destiny was out of their hands. That He was going where they couldn't come. What Jesus meant was that He was about to go voluntarily to God, His Father. He was going to lay down His life on a cruel cross, but death would not be the end of His work; rather, it would be His earthly completion, leading to His resurrection and His ascension, taking up a heavenly role before His Father, for us. Yes, Jesus is alive, and interceding before His Father for us today!

If you've ever spent any time in church, whether it be at school, at Christmas, or perhaps even at a wedding, the likelihood is you've said, or at least heard, the Nicene Creed. It's a statement that Christians say to affirm what they believe. Its middle paragraph helps us answer our big question – who is Jesus?

> *And [we believe] in one Lord Jesus Christ, the only-begotten Son of God, begotten of the Father before all worlds, God of God, Light of Light, Very God of Very God, begotten, not made, being of one substance with the Father by whom all things were made; who for us men, and for our salvation, came down from*

heaven, and was incarnate by the Holy Spirit of the Virgin Mary, and was made man, and was crucified also for us under Pontius Pilate. He suffered and was buried, and the third day he rose again according to the Scriptures, and ascended into heaven, and [sits] on the right hand of the Father. And he shall come again with glory to judge both the quick and the dead, whose kingdom shall have no end.

Isn't that amazing? There is no 'of course' in that. It is shocking, wonderful truth that God has come to us like this. We don't naturally know God. We certainly don't think of Him coming to earth like this, not as a baby! It is incredible. He has come in the most wonderful way and is looking and longing to forgive us and save us.

If you are reading this today and you're not a Christian – perhaps you've picked it up over the holidays as a quick read, or because a friend has given it to you – then I'm so glad you are reading it. I hope you see how important this question is. Who is Jesus? It is a question of historical and personal importance. It is a question for you.

Jesus came from God and was returning to God. Maybe you are beginning to see that the real Jesus doesn't fit the simple tableau around which so many Christmas traditions and understandings are gathered.

Who is Jesus? It is a question of historical and personal importance. It is a question for you.

But answering the question of Jesus' identity is not enough. We need to consider why Jesus came.

Why did Jesus come?

Jesus talked about His mission and He explained that His work was from God. He didn't come to serve Himself, or to do His own thing, but to do what His heavenly Father asked. All Jesus did was for the glory of His Father. If we are going to understand the real Jesus, that is the most basic motivation we can find in Him, to bring glory to God the Father.

Jesus also came to teach unpleasant truths like that which we can see in verse 7 of that same chapter in John's Gospel: 'The world . . . hates me because I testify that its works are evil.' When you study Jesus carefully you see He is very clear on human sinfulness – what we call depravity; the idea that something is wrong with everybody. He said it earlier in John's Gospel, in chapter 3 verses 19 and 20: 'This is the verdict: light has come into the world, but people loved darkness instead of light because their deeds were evil. Everyone who does evil hates the light, and will not come into the light for fear that their deeds will be exposed.'

The Bible tells us that we are all in big trouble – we are prisoners and need to be set free.

The Bible tells us that we are all in big trouble – we are prisoners and need to be set free. We are people in need. If we're honest with ourselves, we know this is true. We need a Saviour because something is so wrong.

We're all in the same boat.

Christians or skeptics, church goers or sympathizers,

Christmas isn't for tipping our hats to God. No, we need to come as people who know what it means to be needy – to need a Saviour – and to have found that Saviour in Jesus. And this is the good news – Jesus is the Rescuer we need.

Come with me back to the stable birth. Do you remember the message the angels brought Jesus' mother, Mary? Perhaps you've heard it read from the Bible at a Christmas service. The angel said, 'you are to give him the name Jesus, because he will save his people from their sins.' We can read this in Matthew's Gospel, chapter 1 verse 21.

For to us a child is born, to us a son is given, and the government will be on his shoulders.

And so we *can* have *real* joy at Christmas. This is what the prophet Isaiah was talking about in the words that we hear so often read at this time of year:

> *The people walking in darkness have seen a great light; on those living in the land of deep darkness a light has dawned. . . . For to us*

a child is born, to us a son is given, and the government will be on his shoulders. And he will be called Wonderful Counsellor, Mighty God, Everlasting Father, Prince of Peace. Of the increase of his government and peace there will be no end. He will reign on David's throne and over his kingdom, establishing and upholding it with justice and righteousness from that time on and for ever. The zeal of the L*ORD* *Almighty will accomplish this.*

This is why there is joy in Christmas because it is in Christmas that we see the coming of our deliverer – Jesus.

All of this from a tiny baby?

But we have even more long lasting joy because as we look at the cradle of Bethlehem, we do so through the cross of Calvary. Baby Jesus held by the wood of a cradle, later is held to the wood of a cross.

Delivered and delivering.

Jesus held by the wood.

Witnesses on either side.

Mary stood waiting,

quietly gazing,

with great feeling,

on her Son.

The sky dark above.

As at the beginning,

so at the end.

Jesus held by the wood,

delivered and delivering.

Jesus held by the wood.

The scene of Christmas and of Calvary.

Of the cradle and the cross.

We see that this baby grew up and lived a perfect life and died a death in our place as a substitute for us. This baby of Bethlehem was, in a very special way, born to die. The message of Christmas that excites us is here in the last few verses of the Gospel of Mark. What it says totally transforms how we should view Christmas.

> *At noon, darkness came over the whole land until three in the afternoon. And at three in the afternoon Jesus cried out in a loud voice,* Eloi, Eloi, lema sabachthani? *(which means 'My God, my God, why have you forsaken me?')*
>
> *When some of those standing near heard this, they said, 'Listen, he's calling Elijah.' Someone ran, filled a sponge with wine vinegar, put it on a staff, and offered it to Jesus to drink. 'Now leave him alone. Let's see if Elijah comes to take him down,' he said.*

When the centurion, who stood there in front of Jesus, saw how he died, he said, 'Surely this man was the Son of God!'

With a loud cry, Jesus breathed his last.

The curtain of the temple was torn in two from top to bottom. And when the centurion, who stood there in front of Jesus, saw how he died, he said, 'Surely this man was the Son of God!'

Some women were watching from a distance. Among them were Mary Magdalene, Mary the mother of James the younger and of Joseph, and Salome. In Galilee these women had followed him and cared for his needs. Many other women who had come up with him to Jerusalem were also there.

When he learned from the centurion that it was so, he gave the body to Joseph.

It was Preparation Day (that is, the day before the Sabbath). So as evening approached, Joseph of Arimathea, a prominent member of the Council, who was himself waiting for the kingdom of God, went boldly to Pilate and asked for Jesus' body. Pilate was surprised to hear that he was already dead. Summoning the centurion, he asked him if Jesus had already died. When he learned from the centurion that it was so, he gave the body to Joseph. So Joseph bought some linen cloth, took down the body, wrapped it in the linen, and placed it in a tomb cut out of rock. Then he rolled a stone against the entrance of the tomb. Mary Magdalene and Mary the mother of Joseph saw where he was laid.

When the Sabbath was over, Mary Magdalene, Mary the mother of James, and Salome bought spices so that they might go to anoint Jesus' body. Very early on the first day of the week, just after sunrise, they were on their way to the tomb and they asked each other, 'Who will roll the stone away from the entrance of the tomb?'

But when they looked up, they saw the stone, which was very large, had been rolled away. As they entered the tomb, they saw a young man dressed in a white robe sitting on the right side, and they were alarmed.

'Don't be alarmed,' he said. 'You are looking for Jesus the Nazarene, who was crucified. He has risen! He is not here. See the place where they laid him. But go, tell his disciples and Peter, "He is going ahead of you into Galilee. There you will see him, just as he told you."'

Trembling and bewildered, the women went out and fled from the tomb . . . [7]

This baby who grew up is the centre of this story and that is why Christians don't just *have* Christmas, but celebrate it. If you don't understand this, Christmas is like a book of punchlines with no jokes. It is like a series of solutions to problems you have never puzzled over. But, if you have considered your own need for a Saviour, then Christmas is the time when the answer comes. It is a time when we remember that He was born for us. He was born to take away our sin – our

if you have considered your own need for a Saviour, then Christmas is the time when the answer comes. It is a time when we remember that He was born for us.

wrongdoing – by His death on the cross. So just as we keep our presents wrapped up until Christmas morning, then with great delight tear off the paper to reveal the gift, so it is with Jesus – God's gift to humanity – unveiled at that very first Christmas.

So as you read this, like Tom and Sarah with their thingamabob, are you getting the joy of the Christmas season without knowing what it is that is causing the celebration? You are, as it were, standing at the back of the crowd and enjoying the sensation of people being excited, without knowing why. If that's you, I want to encourage you to come forward to look at the manger for yourself, to see the shadow of the cross and the thrill of the empty tomb and the joy of knowing your sins forgiven, your relationship with your Maker restored. Enjoy the beautiful things around Christmas, thank God for family and friends, warmth and food, fun and

Jesus stood and said in a loud voice, 'Let anyone who is thirsty come to me and drink.'

presents, but don't just have Christmas, celebrate the greatest gift of all – Jesus our Saviour.

In John's account of Jesus' life, we see crowds of people ceremonially celebrating a special feast but Jesus stood and said in a loud voice, 'Let anyone who is thirsty come to me and drink. Whoever believes in me, as Scripture has said, rivers of living water will flow from within them.'[8] Jesus called out to the thirsty to come to Him and drink. Jesus was to be the centre of the celebrations. He is the One who brings joy and satisfaction.

Do you thirst? What will satisfy you? You know, when you are really thirsty, nothing will satisfy you but to drink water. Thomas Boston, the Scottish minister said, 'Clothe the thirsty man with scarlet, fill his pockets with gold, yet nothing but drink can satisfy him.'[9] What are you thirsty for today? What is your greatest longing? Do you crave a new start, a chance for a

The greatest news this Christmas is that God longs to forgive, to satisfy and meet the needs of those who are thirsty.

clean slate, someone to forgive you? Do you desire God and His forgiveness?

The greatest news this Christmas is that God longs to forgive, to satisfy and meet the needs of those who are thirsty. We can pray to Him and He will meet our truest and deepest need.

The Bible says we have all fallen short of God's perfect standard. That is, we have *all* got it wrong, and offended God and other people in what we think, say and do. The Bible says God is perfect. He has never done anything wrong. He's never had to say sorry – the Bible calls this holy. And because of this He cannot ignore the wrong we do. It wouldn't be right and just to simply sweep it under the carpet. So we must face God as Judge.

We are only made right with God by trusting Jesus, not by our own good works. We simply cannot make ourselves 'right' in God's eyes.

But He is also loving and does not want us to be eternally separated from Him. So He sent His Son, Jesus, to be a sacrifice for us, to take upon Himself the punishment we deserve in His death on the cross.

When Jesus had given His life, after three days, God raised Him to life again, showing that He had accepted the sacrifice. This means that anyone who turns to Jesus and trusts in Him will be forgiven. We are only made right with God by trusting Jesus, not by our own good works. We simply cannot make ourselves 'right' in God's eyes. But Jesus can.

The thingamabob in the story of Tom and Sarah was nice on the mantel, but it was meant for the clock and it brought joy there it could never bring on the mantel. The baby of Christmas is nice, but He was meant for the cross. He was born to die and you'll only understand Him in light of that. When you find the cross in Christmas, you will find the reason for the baby and the reason for the celebration and a reason for your life. You'll find the reason for Christians and to be able to sing 'Joy to the world, the Lord is come!'[10]

John 7

1 After this, Jesus went around in Galilee. He did not want to go about in Judea because the Jewish leaders there were looking for a way to kill him. 2 But when the Jewish Festival of Tabernacles was near, 3 Jesus' brothers said to him, 'Leave Galilee and go to Judea, so that your disciples there may see the works you do. 4 No one who wants to become a public figure acts in secret. Since you are doing these things, show yourself to the world.' 5 For even his own brothers did not believe in him.

6 Therefore Jesus told them, 'My time is not yet here; for you any time will do. 7 The world cannot hate you, but it hates me because I testify that its works are evil. 8 You go to the festival. I am not going up to this festival, because my time has not yet fully come.' 9 After he had said this, he stayed in Galilee.

10 However, after his brothers had left for the festival, he went also, not publicly, but in secret. 11 Now at the festival the Jewish leaders were watching for Jesus and asking, 'Where is he?'

12 Among the crowds there was widespread whispering about him. Some said, 'He is a good man.'

Others replied, 'No, he deceives the people.' 13 But no one would say anything publicly about him for fear of the leaders.

14 Not until halfway through the festival did Jesus go up to the temple courts and begin to teach. 15 The Jews there were amazed and asked, 'How did this man get such learning without having been taught?'

16 Jesus answered, 'My teaching is not my own. It comes from the one who sent me. 17 Anyone who chooses to do the will of God will find out whether my teaching comes from God or whether I speak on my own. 18 Whoever speaks on their own does so to gain personal glory, but he who seeks the glory of the one who sent him is a man of truth; there is nothing false about him. 19 Has not Moses given you the law? Yet not one of you keeps the law. Why are you trying to kill me?'

20 'You are demon-possessed,' the crowd answered. 'Who is trying to kill you?'

21 Jesus said to them, 'I did one miracle, and you are all amazed. 22 Yet, because Moses gave you circumcision (though actually it did not come from Moses, but from the patriarchs), you circumcise a boy on the Sabbath. 23 Now if a boy can be circumcised on the Sabbath so that the law of Moses may not be broken, why are you angry with me for healing a man's whole body on the Sabbath? 24 Stop judging by mere appearances, but instead judge correctly.'

25 At that point some of the people of Jerusalem began to ask, 'Isn't this the man they are trying to kill? 26 Here he is, speaking publicly, and they are not saying a word to him. Have the authorities really concluded that he is the Messiah? 27 But we know where this man is from; when the Messiah comes, no one will know where he is from.'

28 Then Jesus, still teaching in the temple courts, cried out, 'Yes, you know me, and you know where I am from. I am not here on my own authority, but he who sent me is true. You do not know him, 29 but I know him because I am from him and he sent me.'

30 At this they tried to seize him, but no one laid a hand on him, because his hour had not yet come. 31 Still, many in the crowd believed in him. They said, 'When the Messiah comes, will he perform more signs than this man?'

32 The Pharisees heard the crowd whispering such things about him. Then the chief priests and the Pharisees sent temple guards to arrest him.

33 Jesus said, 'I am with you for only a short time, and then I am going to the one who sent me. 34 You will look for me, but you will not find me; and where I am, you cannot come.'

35 The Jews said to one another, 'Where does this man intend to go that we cannot find him?

Will he go where our people live scattered among the Greeks, and teach the Greeks? 36 What did he mean when he said, "You will look for me, but you will not find me," and "Where I am, you cannot come"?'

37 On the last and greatest day of the festival, Jesus stood and said in a loud voice, 'Let anyone who is thirsty come to me and drink. 38 Whoever believes in me, as Scripture has said, rivers of living water will flow from within them.' 39 By this he meant the Spirit, whom those who believed in him were later to receive. Up to that time the Spirit had not been given, since Jesus had not yet been glorified.

40 On hearing his words, some of the people said, 'Surely this man is the Prophet.'

41 Others said, 'He is the Messiah.'

Still others asked, 'How can the Messiah come from Galilee? 42 Does not Scripture say that the Messiah will come from David's descendants and from Bethlehem, the town where David lived?' 43 Thus the people were divided because of Jesus. 44 Some wanted to seize him, but no one laid a hand on him.

45 Finally the temple guards went back to the chief priests and the Pharisees, who asked them, 'Why didn't you bring him in?'

46 'No one ever spoke the way this man does,' the guards replied.

47 'You mean he has deceived you also?' the Pharisees retorted. 48 'Have any of the rulers or of the Pharisees believed in him? 49 No! But this mob that knows nothing of the law – there is a curse on them.'

50 Nicodemus, who had gone to Jesus earlier

and who was one of their own number, asked, 51 *'Does our law condemn a man without first hearing him to find out what he has been doing?'*

52 *They replied, 'Are you from Galilee, too? Look into it, and you will find that a prophet does not come out of Galilee.'*

Notes

1. Lucinda Franks, writing in *The New York Times*, 23 December 1984. http://www.nytimes.com/1984/12/23/travel/pilgrimage-to-bethlehem.html (accessed 30 August 2013).

2. Isaac Watts (1674–1748), 'Joy to the World'; Charles Wesley (1707–88), 'Hark! the Herald Angels Sing'.

3. You can read this in Mark chapter 10 verse 45 (NIV).

4. See 1 John chapter 4 verse 14.

5. See Luke chapter 2 verse 10.

6. See Isaiah chapter 9 verses 2, 6 and 7.

7. Mark's Gospel, chapter 15 verses 33 to 47, and chapter 16 verses 1 to 8.

8. See John's Gospel, chapter 7 verses 37 and 38.

9. Thomas Boston (1676–1732).

10. Isaac Watts (1674–1748), 'Joy to the World'.